BEST Advice EVER

FALL RIVER PRESS

New York

FALL RIVER PRESS

New York

An Imprint of Sterling Publishing
1166 Avenue of the Americas
New York, NY 10036

Compilation © 2015 Fall River Press

All rights reserved. No part of this publication may be reproduced, stored in a retrieval system, or transmitted, in any form or by any means (electronic, mechanical, photocopying, recording, or otherwise) without prior written permission from the publisher.

Book design by Maria Mann
Jacket design by Laura Palese

ISBN 978-1-4351-5844-3

For information about custom editions, special sales, and premium and corporate purchases, please contact Sterling Special Sales at 800-805-5489 or specialsales@sterlingpublishing.com.

Manufactured in the United States of America

2 4 6 8 10 9 7 5 3 1

www.sterlingpublishing.com

CONTENTS

Introduction	vii
Growing Up	1
It Must Be Love	9
Family Ties	15
Friends Rule	23
Kindness Matters	33
Work Hard to Be Your Best	41
Make Good Choices	49
Give Back	53
Stand Up! Speak Out!	59
Keep Learning	65
All About Technology	77
The Road to Success	83
Life's a Challenge	91
Happiness Is . . .	99
Have Fun!	107
The World We Live In	113
Epic Advice	119
Contributors	130

Special thanks to my son John: thank you for your helpful insights and suggestions for this book—can't wait to read it together!

For my kids, nieces, and nephews—Michael, Elizabeth, William, Jack, Nicole, Will, Conor, Danielle, Molly, John, Patrick, Rachel, Tim, Stephanie, and Emily—you are each amazing and greatly loved.

INTRODUCTION

The last thing anybody wants to do is take advice from a person they don't know, or from a lot of people they don't know. So why read a book filled with nothing but advice from strangers?

Because in this book we have culled quotations from some of the smartest, most creative, and most innovative people in the world. Trust us, you'll want to listen to what they have to say. There is virtually no problem that isn't covered in some way by the quotes here. The selections are grouped according to themes such as challenges, family, friends, fun, good choices, kindness, knowledge, success, technology, and growing up. The speakers include activists, artists, celebrities, inventors, journalists, military leaders, musicians, philosophers, poets, pop stars, presidents, athletes, Supreme Court justices, and writers.

And what do these impressive speakers have to say about life? Kevin Durant reminds us that kindness doesn't mean weakness; Jimmy Fallon says it's okay to be silly; Pope Francis reveals how he tries to make good choices; Derek Jeter reminds us to work hard but to have fun; Pink recalls battles with her mom when she was growing up;

Introduction

Steven Spielberg cautions us about the downside of technology; and Taylor Swift tells us how to deal with haters.

History's heavy hitters, such as Jane Austen, Cicero, and Robert E. Lee, reflect on the meaning of friendship; Helen Keller reveals her secret to happiness; Theodore Roosevelt explains the value of time management; Walt Whitman shares the benefits of giving.

The advice, tips, and wisdom in this book are certainly not limited to teens, and you should consider sharing them with the adults in your life, because, after all, everybody needs good advice. So put down your phone and read on. I hope that the words in these pages will make you think, make you smile, and inspire you to follow your dreams.

—Carol Kelly-Gangi

GROWING UP

Best Advice Ever

Be who you are and say what you feel, because those who mind don't matter and those who matter don't mind.

—Theodor Geisel (a.k.a. Dr. Seuss)

✦ ✦ ✦

It takes courage to grow up and become who you really are.

—e. e. cummings

✦ ✦ ✦

All of my favorite people—people I really trust—none of them were cool in their younger years.

—Taylor Swift

✦ ✦ ✦

I was a sidelines child: never class president, never team captain, never the one with the most valentines in my box.

—Lois Lowry

✦ ✦ ✦

Nothing could be as hard as middle school.

—Zooey Deschanel

Growing Up

I never felt comfortable with myself, because I was never part of the majority. I always felt awkward and shy and on the outside of the momentum of my friends' lives.

—Steven Spielberg

I went through a lot in middle school, and you always try so many different looks and try to be so many different people. I finally realized I'm awkward, I'm lanky, and I'm going to embrace it—make fun of myself and just laugh.

—Ireland Baldwin

I was obsessed with being popular in high school and never achieved it. There's photos from our high school musicals, and I'm comically in the deep background, wearing a beggar's costume.

—Mindy Kaling

It is hard to convince a high school student that he will encounter a lot of problems more difficult than those of algebra and geometry.

—Edgar Watson Howe

Best Advice Ever

I went to a high school reunion a couple years ago and realized that the kids who were the most unusual in high school are the ones who are the most interesting now and the ones who were popular are dull and boring.

—Anderson Cooper

A friend of mine told me he routinely attends all of his high school reunions so he can apologize to every person he mistreated back then. He's now on his fortieth reunion and still apologizing.

—Kareem Abdul-Jabbar

It happens to everyone as they grow up. You find out who you are and what you want, and then you realize that people you've known forever don't see things the way you do. So you keep the wonderful memories, but find yourself moving on.

—Nicholas Sparks

If you've been to high school, chances are you've got a yearbook lying around that's full of enough cringe-worthy quotes and photos to mortify you until your dying day.

—Tina Fey

Growing Up

My mom took all of my behavior personally. Everything I did, she thought it was an act of rebellion against her. But it was just me being me.

—Pink

When I was growing up, there were two things that were unpopular in my house. One was me, and the other was my guitar.

—Bruce Springsteen

Something awful happens to a person who grows up as a creative kid and suddenly finds no creative outlet as an adult.

—Judy Blume

The young always have the same problem—how to rebel and conform at the same time. They have now solved this by defying their parents and copying one another.

—Quentin Crisp

Don't laugh at a youth for his affectations; he is only trying on one face after another to find a face of his own.

—Logan Pearsall Smith

* * *

Growing up is losing some illusions, in order to acquire others.

—Virginia Woolf

* * *

Growing up is after all only the understanding that one's unique and incredible experience is what everyone shares.

—Doris Lessing

* * *

I used to think that when you grew up, you actually stopped growing. How wrong I was.

—Katie Couric

* * *

Grow up, and that is a terribly hard thing to do. It is much easier to skip it and go from one childhood to another.

—F. Scott Fitzgerald

Growing Up

I think that's good that I have to watch how I act and what I say. I think that's a part of growing up.

—Sean Combs

* * *

I've gotten away with a lot in my life. The older you get the more you realize you're not getting away with it, it's taking its toll somewhere. So you try not to put yourself in those situations. Part of the mysterious process called growing up. Some people do that better than others.

—Jon Hamm

* * *

There was no respect for youth when I was young, and now that I am old, there is no respect for age—I missed it coming and going.

—J. B. Priestly

* * *

Where I was born and where and how I have lived is unimportant. It is what I have done with where I have been that should be of interest.

—Georgia O'Keeffe

Best Advice Ever

Real maturity is the ability to imagine the humanity of every person as fully as you believe in your own humanity.

—Tobias Wolff

IT MUST BE LOVE

Best Advice Ever

Love is of all passions the strongest, for it attacks simultaneously the head, the heart, and the senses.

—Lao Tzu

* * *

Love stretches your heart and makes you big inside.

—Margaret Walker

* * *

Love is the only force capable of transforming an enemy into a friend.

—Martin Luther King, Jr.

* * *

Love is a condition in which the happiness of another person is essential to your own.

—Robert A. Heinlein

* * *

The essence of love is kindness.

—Robert Louis Stevenson

It Must Be Love

If you would be loved, love and be lovable.
—**Benjamin Franklin**

You know you're in love when you don't want to fall asleep because reality is finally better than your dreams.
—**Theodor Geisel**

Love makes your soul crawl out from its hiding place.
—**Zora Neale Hurston**

Love is a choice you make from moment to moment.
—**Barbara De Angelis**

We are most alive when we're in love.
—**John Updike**

The magic of first love is our ignorance that it can ever end.
—**Benjamin Disraeli**

Best Advice Ever

It's a very dangerous state. You are inclined to recklessness and kind of tune out the rest of your life and everything that's been important to you. It's actually not all that pleasurable. I don't know who the hell wants to get in a situation where you can't bear an hour without somebody's company.

—Colin Firth

The loss of young first love is so painful that it borders on the ludicrous.

—Maya Angelou

You know it's love when all you want is that person to be happy, even if you're not part of their happiness.

—Julia Roberts

The greater your capacity to love, the greater your capacity to feel the pain.

—Jennifer Aniston

It Must Be Love

'Tis better to have loved and lost
Than never to have loved at all

—Alfred, Lord Tennyson

* * *

The best way to mend a broken heart is time and girlfriends.

—Gwyneth Paltrow

* * *

Too many girls rush into relationships because of the fear of being single, then start making compromises, and losing their identity. Don't do that.

—Katy Perry

* * *

I love who I am, and I encourage other people to love and embrace who they are. But it definitely wasn't easy—it took me a while.

—Serena Williams

Best Advice Ever

The one thing we can never get enough of is love. And the one thing we never give enough of is love.

—**Henry Miller**

* * *

Love is patient and kind; love is not jealous or boastful; it is not arrogant or rude. Love does not insist on its own way; it is not irritable or resentful; it does not rejoice at wrong, but rejoices in the right. Love bears all things, believes all things, hopes all things.

—**St. Paul**

* * *

Keep love in your heart. A life without it is like a sunless garden when the flowers are dead. The consciousness of loving and being loved brings a warmth and richness to life that nothing else can bring.

—**Oscar Wilde**

FAMILY TIES

Best Advice Ever

The family. We were a strange little band of characters trudging through life sharing diseases and toothpaste, coveting one another's desserts, hiding shampoo, borrowing money, locking each other out of our rooms, inflicting pain and kissing to heal it in the same instant, loving, laughing, defending, and trying to figure out the common thread that bound us all together.

—Erma Bombeck

* * *

You don't really understand human nature unless you know why a child on a merry-go-round will wave at his parents every time around—and why his parents will always wave back.

—William D. Tammeus

* * *

It is my pleasure that my children are free and happy, and unrestrained by parental tyranny. Love is the chain whereby to bind a child to its parents.

—Abraham Lincoln

Family Ties

My relationship with my mom is really the single most profound relationship that I've ever had in my life.

—Mindy Kaling

My father gave me the greatest gift anyone can give another person, he believed in me.

—Jim Valvano

Above all, children need our unconditional love, whether they succeed or make mistakes; when life is easy and when life is tough.

—Barack Obama

Loving a child doesn't mean giving in to all his whims; to love him is to bring out the best in him, to teach him to love what is difficult.

—Nadia Boulanger

Best Advice Ever

You made us believe, you kept us off the street. You put clothes on our backs, food on the table. When you didn't eat, you made sure we ate. You went to sleep hungry. You sacrificed for us. You're the real MVP.

—Kevin Durant, speaking about his mom

My friends ask me why I still live with my family, but I feel comfortable there. We've all been through so much together.

—Shaun White

Mummy herself has told us that she looked upon us more as her friends than her daughters. Now that is all very fine, but still, a friend can't take a mother's place.

—Anne Frank

To an adolescent, there is nothing in the world more embarrassing than a parent.

—Dave Barry

Family Ties

My parents were kind of over protective people. Me and my sister had to play in the backyard all the time. They bought us bikes for Christmas but wouldn't let us ride in the street, we had to ride in the backyard. Another Christmas, my dad got me a basketball hoop and put it in the middle of the lawn! You can't dribble on grass.

—Jimmy Fallon

My mother had a great deal of trouble with me, but I think she enjoyed it.

—Mark Twain

Adolescence is a period of rapid changes. Between the ages of 12 and 17, for example, a parent ages as much as 20 years.

—Anonymous

The best way to keep children at home is to make the home atmosphere pleasant, and let the air out of the tires.

—Dorothy Parker

Best Advice Ever

When I was a boy of fourteen, my father was so ignorant I could hardly stand to have the old man around. But when I got to be twenty-one, I was astonished at how much the old man had learned in seven years.

—**Mark Twain**

When our relatives are at home, we have to think of all their good points or it would be impossible to endure them.

—**George Bernard Shaw**

The great advantage of living in a large family is that early lesson of life's essential unfairness.

—**Nancy Mitford**

The other night I ate at a real nice family restaurant. Every table had an argument going.

—**George Carlin**

Family Ties

If you have only one smile in you, give it to the people you love. Don't be surly at home, then go out in the street and start grinning "Good morning" at total strangers.

—Maya Angelou

* * *

There is no doubt that it is around the family and the home that all the greatest virtues, the most dominating virtues of human society, are created, strengthened and maintained.

—Winston Churchill

* * *

One of the oldest human needs is having someone to wonder where you are when you don't come home at night.

—Margaret Mead

* * *

If you look deeply into the palm of your hand, you will see your parents and all generations of your ancestors. All of them are alive in this moment. Each is present in your body. You are the continuation of each of these people.

—Thich Nhat Hanh

Best Advice Ever

Let us make one point, that we meet each other with a smile, when it is difficult to smile. Smile at each other, make time for each other in your family.

—Mother Teresa

* * *

In every conceivable manner, the family is the link to our past, bridge to our future.

—Alex Haley

FRIENDS RULE

Best Advice Ever

What is a friend? A single soul dwelling in two bodies.

—Aristotle

A friend is a gift you give yourself.

—Robert Louis Stevenson

They cherish each other's hopes. They are kind to each other's dreams.

—Henry David Thoreau

The only way to have a friend is to be one.

—Ralph Waldo Emerson

You can make more friends in two months by becoming interested in other people than you can in two years by trying to get other people interested in you.

—Dale Carnegie

Friends Rule

The best part about having true friends is that you can go months without seeing them and they'll still be there for you and act as if you'd never left!

—Ariana Grande

* * *

A true friend is one who overlooks your failures and tolerates your success!

—Doug Larson

* * *

One friend with whom you have a lot in common is better than three with whom you struggle to find things to talk about.

—Mindy Kaling

* * *

Each friend represents a world in us, a world possibly not born until they arrive, and it is only by this meeting that a new world is born.

—Anaïs Nin

Best Advice Ever

It is one of the blessings of old friends that you can afford to be stupid with them.

—Ralph Waldo Emerson

* * *

Trust is hard to come by. That's why my circle is small and tight. I'm kind of funny about making new friends.

—Eminem

* * *

Be courteous to all, but intimate with few, and let those few be well tried before you give them your confidence.

—George Washington

* * *

Never do a wrong thing to make a friend or keep one.

—Robert E. Lee

* * *

I would rather walk with a friend in the dark than walk alone in the light.

—Helen Keller

Friends Rule

True friendship consists not in the multitude of friends, but in their worth and value.

—Ben Jonson

* * *

Friendship marks a life even more deeply than love. Love risks degenerating into obsession, friendship is never anything but sharing.

—Elie Wiesel

* * *

Friendship with oneself is all important because without it one cannot be friends with anybody else in the world.

—Eleanor Roosevelt

* * *

The best relationships develop out of friendships.

—Diane Keaton

* * *

Friendship is the finest balm for the pangs of despised love.

—Jane Austen

Best Advice Ever

Friendship makes prosperity more shining and lessens adversity by dividing and sharing it.

—Cicero

Friendship is the hardest thing in the world to explain. It's not something you learn in school. But if you haven't learned the meaning of friendship, you really haven't learned anything.

—Muhammad Ali

Lots of people want to ride with you in the limo, but what you want is someone who will take the bus with you when the limo breaks down.

—Oprah Winfrey

The proper office of a friend is to side with you when you are wrong. Nearly anybody will side with you when you are right.

—Mark Twain

Friends Rule

The friend in my adversity I shall always cherish most. I can better trust those who helped to relieve the gloom of my dark hours than those who are so ready to enjoy with me the sunshine of my prosperity.

—Ulysses S. Grant

* * *

Do good to those who hate you and turn their ill will to friendship.

—Abraham Lincoln

* * *

What a delight it is to make friends with someone you have despised!

—Colette

* * *

To keep up and improve Friendship, thou must be willing to receive a Kindness, as well as to do one.

—Thomas Fuller

Best Advice Ever

In everyone's life, at some time, our inner fire goes out. It is then burst into flame by an encounter with another human being. We should all be thankful for those people who rekindle the inner spirit.

—Albert Schweitzer

* * *

We are all travelers in the wilderness of this world, and the best we can find in our travels is an honest friend.

—Robert Louis Stevenson

* * *

No road is long with good company.

—Turkish proverb

* * *

I felt it shelter to speak to you.

—Emily Dickinson

* * *

The shortest distance between new friends is a smile.

—Author unknown

Friends Rule

Friendship is the inexpressible comfort of feeling safe with a person, having neither to weigh thoughts nor measure words.

—George Eliot

* * *

Don't walk behind me; I may not lead. Don't walk in front of me; I may not follow. Just walk beside me and be my friend.

—Albert Camus

* * *

Let us be grateful to people who make us happy; they are the charming gardeners who make our souls blossom.

—Marcel Proust

* * *

Life is nothing without friendship.

—Cicero

KINDNESS MATTERS

Best Advice Ever

No act of kindness, no matter how small, is ever wasted.

—Aesop

✦ ✦ ✦

Be kind, for everyone you meet is fighting a harder battle.

—Plato

✦ ✦ ✦

Three things in human life are important: the first is to be kind; the second is to be kind; and the third is to be kind.

—Henry James

✦ ✦ ✦

Too often we underestimate the power of a touch, a smile, a kind word, a listening ear, an honest compliment, or the smallest act of caring, all of which have the potential to turn a life around.

—Leo Buscaglia

✦ ✦ ✦

No kind action ever stops with itself. One kind action leads to another. Good example is followed. A single act of kindness throws out roots in all directions, and the roots spring up and make new trees.

—Amelia Earhart

Kindness Matters

I just want to let people know that being kind is not a sign of weakness. . . . That's how I approach the game. If you see me play, I'm barking at guys, I'm talking trash, I'm being physical. But at the same time, if you fall on the ground, I'll help you up, and after the game we'll talk as friends. So it's not a weakness to be a kind person. Everybody always says nice guys finish last, but I'm trying to change that.

—Kevin Durant

* * *

Tenderness and kindness are not signs of weakness and despair, but manifestations of strength and resolution.

—Kahlil Gibran

* * *

Being kind to others is a way of being good to yourself.

—Rabbi Harold Kushner

* * *

You cannot shake hands with a clenched fist.

—Indira Gandhi

Best Advice Ever

If you judge people, you have no time to love them.

—**Mother Teresa**

✦ ✦ ✦

We've got a budget deficit that's important, we've got a trade deficit that's critical, but what I worry about most is our empathy deficit. When I speak to students, I tell them that one of the most important things we can do is to look through somebody else's eyes.

—**Barack Obama**

✦ ✦ ✦

Empathy is seeing with the eyes of another, listening with the ears of another and feeling with the heart of another.

—**Alfred Adler**

✦ ✦ ✦

I learned compassion from being discriminated against. Everything bad that's ever happened to me has taught me compassion.

—**Ellen DeGeneres**

Kindness Matters

I speak to everyone in the same way, whether he is the garbage man or the president of the university.

—Albert Einstein

* * *

If something uncharitable is said in your presence, either speak in favor of the absent, or withdraw, or, if possible, stop the conversation.

—St. John Vianney

* * *

You are not only responsible for what you say, but also for what you do not say.

—Martin Luther

* * *

I've learned that people will forget what you said, people will forget what you did, but people will never forget how you made them feel.

—Maya Angelou

Best Advice Ever

Wherever there is a human in need, there is an opportunity for kindness and to make a difference.

—Kevin Heath

* * *

Gentleness, self-sacrifice and generosity are the exclusive possession of no one race or religion.

—Mahatma Gandhi

* * *

No matter what happens in life, be good to people. Being good to people is a wonderful legacy to leave behind.

—Taylor Swift

* * *

We think too much and feel too little. More than machinery, we need humanity. More than cleverness, we need kindness and gentleness.

—Charlie Chaplin

* * *

A kind word is like a spring day.

—Russian proverb

Kindness Matters

Let us make one point, that we meet each other with a smile, when it is difficult to smile. Smile at each other, make time for each other in your family.

—Mother Teresa

What do we live for, if it is not to make life less difficult for each other?

—George Eliot

WORK HARD TO BE YOUR BEST

Best Advice Ever

I never had a policy; I have just tried to do my very best each and every day.

—Abraham Lincoln

* * *

Bodily vigor is good, and vigor of intellect is even better, but far above is character.

—Theodore Roosevelt

* * *

Character building begins in our infancy and continues until death.

—Eleanor Roosevelt

* * *

Parents can only give good advice or put them on the right paths, but the final forming of a person's character lies in their own hands.

—Anne Frank

* * *

Have a belief in yourself that is bigger than anyone's disbelief.

—August Wilson

Work Hard to Be Your Best

I believe in my game, and I believe in me. At the end of the day, I'm my biggest fan. Well, maybe my dad. But other than that, you have to be your biggest fan. I'm working on trying to stay positive.

—Serena Williams

I believe I've always been a big believer in equality. No one has ever been able to tell me I couldn't do something because I was a girl.

—Anne Hathaway

There may be people who have more talent than you, but there's no excuse for anyone to work harder than you do—and I believe that.

—Derek Jeter

I can accept failure, but I can't accept not trying.

—Michael Jordan

Best Advice Ever

Once you learn to quit, it becomes a habit.

—Vince Lombardi

You miss 100 percent of the shots you don't take.

—Wayne Gretzky

Champions aren't made in the gyms. Champions are made from something they have deep inside them—a desire, a dream, a vision.

—Muhammad Ali

Champions keep playing until they get it right.

—Billie Jean King

I've worked too hard and too long to let anything stand in the way of my goals. I will not let my teammates down and I will not let myself down.

—Mia Hamm

Work Hard to Be Your Best

People don't understand that when I grew up, I was never the most talented. I was never the biggest. I was never the fastest. I certainly was never the strongest. The only thing I had was my work ethic, and that's been what has gotten me this far.

—Tiger Woods

* * *

Talent is cheaper than table salt. What separates the talented individual from the successful one is a lot of hard work.

—Stephen King

* * *

Laziness may appear attractive, but work gives satisfaction.

—Anne Frank

* * *

Work is and always has been my salvation and I thank the Lord for it.

—Louisa May Alcott

Best Advice Ever

My grandfather once told me that there are two kinds of people: those who work and those who take the credit. He told me to try to be in the first group; there was less competition there.

—Indira Gandhi

* * *

It takes less time to do a thing right, than it does to explain why you did it wrong.

—Henry Wadsworth Longfellow

* * *

If you think your teacher is tough, wait till you get a boss.

—Bill Gates

* * *

Do the best you can in every task, no matter how unimportant it may seem at the time.

—Sandra Day O'Connor

* * *

Perfection is not attainable. But if we chase perfection, we can catch excellence.

—Vince Lombardi

Work Hard to Be Your Best

I do know one thing about me: I don't measure myself by others' expectations or let others define my worth.

—Sonia Sotomayor

What other people think of you is not your business. If you start to make that business your business, you will be offended for the rest of your life.

—Deepak Chopra

There is something inherently valuable about being a misfit. It's not to say that every person who has artistic talent was a social outcast, but there is definitely a value for identifying yourself differently and being proud that you are different.

—Daniel Radcliffe

If there's any message to my work, it is ultimately that it's okay to be different, that it's good to be different, that we should question ourselves before we pass judgment on someone who looks different, behaves different, talks different, is a different color.

—Johnny Depp

Best Advice Ever

I want women to know that it's okay. That you can be whatever size you are and you can be beautiful inside and out. We're always told what's beautiful, and what's not, and that's not right.

—Serena Williams

I think it's very important that we instill in our kids that it has nothing to do with their name or their situation that they're growing up in; it has to do with who they are as an individual.

—Melinda Gates

If we all did the things we are capable of doing, we would literally astound ourselves.

—Thomas Edison

MAKE GOOD CHOICES

Best Advice Ever

When someone makes a decision, he is really diving into a strong current that will carry him to places he had never dreamed of when he first made the decision.

—Paulo Coelho, *The Alchemist*

* * *

The strongest principle of growth lies in the human choice.

—George Eliot

* * *

I believe without a single shadow of a doubt that it is necessary for young people to learn to make choices. Learning to make right choices is the only way they will survive in an increasingly frightening world.

—Lois Lowry

* * *

Too often in life, something happens and we blame other people for us not being happy or satisfied or fulfilled. So the point is, we all have choices, and we make the choice to accept people or situations or to not accept situations.

—Tom Brady

* * *

To find yourself, think for yourself.

—Socrates

Make Good Choices

I am happy that the young girls have a lot more choices these days and an opportunity to feel better about themselves.

—Mia Hamm

＊ ＊ ＊

When you know better you do better.

—Maya Angelou

＊ ＊ ＊

As long as there remains a drop of blood in our body there will be a struggle between right and wrong.

—St. Padre Pio

＊ ＊ ＊

If you don't stick to your values when they're being tested, they're not values: they're hobbies.

—Jon Stewart

＊ ＊ ＊

I am always wary of decisions made hastily. I am always wary of the first decision, that is, the first thing that comes to my mind if I have to make a decision. This is usually the wrong thing. I have to wait and assess, looking deep into myself, taking the necessary time.

—Pope Francis

Best Advice Ever

To make the right choices in life, you have to get in touch with your soul. To do this, you need to experience solitude, which most people are afraid of, because in the silence you hear the truth and know the solutions.

—Deepak Chopra

* * *

Life is the sum of all your choices.

—Albert Camus

* * *

It is our choices . . . that show what we truly are, far more than our abilities.

—J.K. Rowling, *Harry Potter and the Chamber of Secrets*

* * *

May your choices reflect your hopes, not your fears.

—Nelson Mandela

GIVE BACK

Best Advice Ever

The meaning of life is to find your gift. The purpose of life is to give it away.

—**Pablo Picasso**

* * *

And so, my fellow Americans: ask not what your country can do for you—ask what you can do for your country.

—**John F. Kennedy**

* * *

If you think about what you ought to do for other people, your character will take care of itself.

—**Woodrow Wilson**

* * *

I've been giving back since I was a teen, handing out turkeys at Thanksgiving and handing out toys at toys drives for Christmas. It's very important to give back as a youth. It's as simple as helping an old lady across the street or giving up your seat on the bus for someone who is pregnant.

—**Queen Latifah**

Give Back

Sometimes when we are generous in small, barely detectable ways it can change someone else's life forever.

—Margaret Cho

* * *

The habit of giving only enhances the desire to give.

—Walt Whitman

* * *

It's not how much we give but how much love we put into giving.

—Mother Teresa

* * *

The purpose of my life is to see every child go to school and get education . . . I speak for those children whose right to safety, health and quality education has been snatched from them. I speak for the 66 million girls who are out of school.

—Malala Yousafzai

Best Advice Ever

At the end of the day, it's not about what you have or even what you've accomplished. It's about what you've done with those accomplishments. It's about who you've lifted up, who you've made better. It's about what you've given back.

—Denzel Washington

I will continue to distribute blankets, sleeping bags, warm clothing and food on a regular basis, in the hope that my modest efforts will give some comfort to those people we are able to help.

—Mohamed Al-Fayed

Acts of sacrifice and decency without regard to what's in it for you create ripple effects. Ones that lift up families and communities, that spread opportunity and boost our economy.

—Barack Obama

Everyone has the power for greatness, not for fame, but greatness, because greatness is determined by service.

—Martin Luther King, Jr.

Give Back

Service is the rent we pay for being. It is the very purpose of life and not something you do in your spare time.

—Marian Wright Edelman

* * *

Giving frees us from the familiar territory of our own needs by opening our mind to the unexplained worlds occupied by the needs of others.

—Barbara Bush

* * *

All I can do is be the best me that I can. And live life with some gusto. Giving back is a big part of that.

—Michelle Obama

* * *

With a generation of younger folks who have thrived on the success of their companies, there is a big opportunity for many of us to give back earlier in our lifetime and see the impact of our philanthropic efforts.

—Mark Zuckerberg

Best Advice Ever

No one has ever become poor by giving.

—Anne Frank

You give but little when you give of your possessions. It is when you give of yourself that you truly give.

—Kahlil Gibran

The greatest gift is a portion of thyself.

—Ralph Waldo Emerson

Life's persistent and most urgent question is "What are you doing for others?"

—Martin Luther King, Jr.

STAND UP! SPEAK OUT!

Best Advice Ever

Standing for right when it is unpopular is a true test of moral character.

—Margaret Chase Smith

* * *

Courage is fire, and bullying is smoke.

—Benjamin Disraeli

* * *

I abhor injustice and bullying by the strong at the expense of the weak.

—Theodore Roosevelt

* * *

At the end of the day, no one deserves to be bullied. I was bullied and I had to leave public school because of it. When you deal with bullies, I think it's important to have a confidant in your life. I have a friend that I go to and I just vent about everything to her!

—Demi Lovato

Stand Up! Speak Out!

Never be bullied into silence. Never allow yourself to be made a victim. Accept no one's definition of your life; define yourself.

—Harvey Fierstein

* * *

I got made fun of constantly in high school. That's what built my character. That's what makes you who you are. When you get made fun of, when people point out your weaknesses, that's just another opportunity for you to rise above.

—Zac Efron

* * *

People who are feeling bullied and people who feel like outsiders should talk to their parents and guardians about finding a place with likeminded people where they can feel accepted. That's what I needed, and that's what I found with musical theater.

—Nick Jonas

Best Advice Ever

I was bullied and it's hard, you feel like high school's never going to be over. It's four years of your life and you just have to remember the person picking on you has their own problems and their own issues.

—Megan Fox

* * *

I allowed myself to be bullied because I was scared and didn't know how to defend myself. I was bullied until I prevented a new student from being bullied. By standing up for him, I learned to stand up for myself.

—Jackie Chan

* * *

People talk about bullying, but you can be your own bully in some ways. You can be the person who is standing in the way of your success, and that was the case for me.

—Katy Perry

* * *

Most comedy is based on getting a laugh at somebody else's expense. And I find that that's just a form of bullying in a major way. So I want to be an example that you can be funny and be kind, and make people laugh without hurting somebody else's feelings.

—Ellen DeGeneres

Stand Up! Speak Out!

It takes a great deal of bravery to stand up to our enemies, but just as much to stand up to our friends.

—J.K. Rowling, *Harry Potter and the Sorcerer's Stone*

* * *

It is not easy to stand up against your constituents or your friends or colleagues or your community and take a tough stand for something you believe is right. Because you always want to keep working and live to fight another battle and it might cost you your career.

—Caroline Kennedy

* * *

When you hear people making hateful comments, stand up to them. Point out what a waste it is to hate, and you could open their eyes.

—Taylor Swift

* * *

The world is a dangerous place; not because of those who do evil, but because of those who look on and do nothing.

—Albert Einstein

Best Advice Ever

The opposite of love is not hate, it's indifference.

—Elie Wiesel

If you are neutral in situations of injustice, you have chosen the side of the oppressor. If an elephant has its foot on the tail of a mouse, and you say that you are neutral, the mouse will not appreciate your neutrality.

—Desmond Tutu

To ignore evil is to become an accomplice to it.

—Martin Luther King, Jr.

You have enemies? Good. That means you've stood up for something, sometime in your life.

—Winston Churchill

KEEP LEARNING

Best Advice Ever

A mind is a fire to be kindled, not a vessel to be filled.

—Plutarch

* * *

Home is a child's first and most important classroom.

—Hillary Clinton

* * *

My parents taught me how to listen to everybody before I made up my own mind. When you listen, you learn. You absorb like a sponge—and your life becomes so much better than when you are just trying to be listened to all the time.

—Steven Spielberg

* * *

Part of teaching is helping students learn how to tolerate ambiguity, consider possibilities, and ask questions that are unanswerable.

—Sara Lawrence-Lightfoot

We have to teach our boys the rules of equality and respect, so that as they grow up gender equality becomes a natural way of life. And we have to teach our girls that they can reach as high as humanly possible.

—Beyoncé

Education is not the filling of a pail, but the lighting of a fire.

—William Butler Yeats

I think education is power. I think that being able to communicate with people is power. One of my main goals on the planet is to encourage people to empower themselves.

—Oprah Winfrey

Education was the most important value in our home when I was growing up. People don't always realize that my parents shared a sense of intellectual curiosity and a love of reading and of history.

—Caroline Kennedy

Without education, you are not going anywhere in this world.

—Malcolm X

The highest result of education is tolerance.

—Helen Keller

To educate a person in mind and not in morals is to educate a menace to society.

—Theodore Roosevelt

Intelligence plus character—that is the goal of true education.

—Martin Luther King, Jr.

The imagination should be allowed a certain amount of time to browse around.

—Thomas Merton

Keep Learning

He who has imagination without learning has wings and no feet.

—Joseph Joubert

Imagination is more important than knowledge. Knowledge is limited. Imagination encircles the world.

—Albert Einstein

I am always ready to learn, although I do not always like being taught.

—Winston Churchill

Everywhere, we learn only from those whom we love.

—Goethe

Learn by doing.

—Proverb

Best Advice Ever

I am always doing that which I cannot do, in order that I may learn how to do it.

—Pablo Picasso

Anyone who stops learning is old, whether at twenty or eighty. Anyone who keeps learning stays young. The greatest thing in life is to keep your mind young.

—Henry Ford

We teach what we need to learn and write what we need to know.

—Gloria Steinem

Knowledge is power.

—Francis Bacon

Knowledge is love and light and vision.

—Helen Keller

Keep Learning

Knowledge will forever govern ignorance; and a people who mean to be their own governors must arm themselves with the power which knowledge gives.

—James Madison

Knowledge is of no value unless you put it into practice.

—Anton Chekhov

The dumbest people I know are those who know it all.

—Malcolm Forbes

A little learning is a dangerous thing.

—Alexander Pope

The simple act of paying attention can take you a long way.

—Keanu Reeves

Best Advice Ever

I really had a lot of dreams when I was a kid and I think a great deal of that grew out of the fact that I had a chance to read a lot.

—Bill Gates

* * *

Books are the quietest and most constant of friends; they are the most accessible and wisest of counsellors, and the most patient of teachers.

—Charles William Eliot

* * *

I'm a big believer in pairing classics with contemporary literature, so students have the opportunity to see that literature is not a cold, dead thing that happened once but instead a vibrant mode of storytelling that's been with us a long time—and will be with us, I hope, for a long time to come.

—John Green

* * *

Learning is a treasure that will follow its owner everywhere.

—Chinese proverb

Keep Learning

If you read something online that piques your curiosity, look it up. Verify it. It might be right, it might be wrong. That doesn't matter. Either way, you'll be learning.

—Lorde

I read to entertain myself, to educate myself, as a way to enlighten myself—as a way to challenge my beliefs about myself.

—LeVar Burton

The love of learning, the sequestered nooks, and all the sweet serenity of books.

—Henry Wadsworth Longfellow

I am a part of everything that I have read.

—Theodore Roosevelt

Best Advice Ever

I was brought up to believe that the only thing worth doing was to add to the sum of accurate information in the world.

—Margaret Mead

* * *

Schooling is what happens inside the walls of the school, some of which is educational. Education happens everywhere, and it happens from the moment a child is born—and some people say before—until a person dies.

—Sara Lawrence-Lightfoot

* * *

I have never let my schooling interfere with my education.

—Mark Twain

* * *

I had many teachers that were great, positive role models and taught me to be a good person and stand up and be a good man. A lot of the principles they taught me still affect how I act sometimes and it's 30 years later.

—Kevin James

I'm going to college. I don't care if it ruins my career. I'd rather be smart than a movie star.

—Natalie Portman

Four years was enough of Harvard. I still had a lot to learn but had been given the liberating notion that now I could teach myself.

—John Updike

Experience: that most brutal of teachers. But you learn, my God do you learn.

—C. S. Lewis

Think wrongly, if you please, but in all cases think for yourself.

—Doris Lessing

Best Advice Ever

The empires of the future are the empires of the mind.

—Winston Churchill

* * *

The important thing is not to stop questioning.

—Albert Einstein

* * *

Life is my college. May I graduate well, and earn some honors!

—Louisa May Alcott

ALL ABOUT TECHNOLOGY

Best Advice Ever

The number one benefit of information technology is that it empowers people to do what they want to do. It lets people be creative. It lets people be productive. It lets people learn things they didn't think they could learn before, and so in a sense it is all about potential.

—Steve Ballmer

Technology can be our best friend, and technology can also be the biggest party pooper of our lives. It interrupts our own story, interrupts our ability to have a thought or a daydream, to imagine something wonderful, because we're too busy bridging the walk from the cafeteria back to the office on the cell phone.

—Steven Spielberg

Once a new technology rolls over you, if you're not part of the steamroller, you're part of the road.

—Stewart Brand

Computers are useless. They can only give you answers.

—Pablo Picasso

All About Technology

Technology is nothing. What's important is that you have a faith in people, that they're basically good and smart, and if you give them tools, they'll do wonderful things with them.

—Steve Jobs

* * *

Technology is just a tool. In terms of getting the kids working together and motivating them, the teacher is the most important.

—Bill Gates

* * *

I got my first computer in the 6th grade or so. As soon as I got it, I was interested in finding out how it worked and how the programs worked and then figuring out how to write programs at just deeper and deeper levels within the system.

—Mark Zuckerberg

* * *

Never let a computer know you're in a hurry.

—Anonymous

Best Advice Ever

The Internet is just a world passing notes around a classroom.

—Jon Stewart

* * *

There is much pleasure to be gained from useless knowledge.

—Bertrand Russell

* * *

Where is all the knowledge we lost with information?

—T. S. Eliot

* * *

Every once in a while a revolutionary product comes along that changes everything. It's very fortunate if you can work on just one of these in your career. . . . Apple's been very fortunate in that it's introduced a few of these.

—Steve Jobs

* * *

I just believed. I believed that the technology would change people's lives. I believed putting real identity online—putting technology behind real identity—was the missing link.

—Sheryl Sandberg

All About Technology

My cell phone is my best friend. It's my lifeline to the outside world.

—Carrie Underwood

* * *

With the evolution of social media that includes blogging, Facebook, and Twitter, who and how information is delivered has changed tremendously. The landscape for news is a different place, and people have to accept that.

—Michael Eric Dyson

* * *

The Internet is so big, so powerful and pointless that for some people it is a complete substitute for life.

—Andrew Brown

* * *

On Twitter we get excited if someone follows us. In real life we get really scared and run away.

—Author unknown

* * *

You'd be surprised how difficult it is relinquish a cell phone.

—Adrien Brody

Best Advice Ever

There will still be things that machines cannot do. They will not produce great art or great literature or great philosophy; they will not be able to discover the secret springs of happiness in the human heart; they will know nothing of love and friendship.

—Bertrand Russell

The most technologically efficient machine that man has ever invented is the book.

—Northrop Frye

Please, no matter how we advance technologically, please don't abandon the book. There is nothing in our material world more beautiful than the book.

—Patti Smith

Man is still the most extraordinary computer of all.

—John F. Kennedy

THE ROAD TO SUCCESS

Best Advice Ever

There are no secrets to success. It is a result of preparation, hard work, and learning from failure.

—Colin Powell

Success is liking yourself, liking what you do, and liking how you do it.

—Maya Angelou

Success is a state of mind. If you want success, start thinking of yourself as a success.

—Joyce Brothers

Success is a journey, not a destination. The doing is often more important than the outcome.

—Arthur Ashe

Success is a lousy teacher. It seduces smart people into thinking they can't lose.

—Bill Gates

The Road to Success

Try not to become a person of success, but rather try to become a person of value.

—Albert Einstein

* * *

I'm convinced that about half of what separates the successful entrepreneurs from the non-successful ones is pure perseverance.

—Steve Jobs

* * *

If we look back on our past life we shall see that one of its most usual experiences is that we have been helped by our mistakes.

—Winston Churchill

* * *

Everybody has setbacks in their life, and everybody falls short of whatever goals they might set for themselves. That's part of living and coming to terms with who you are as a person.

—Hillary Clinton

Best Advice Ever

Obstacles are those frightful things you see when you take your eyes off your goal.

—Henry Ford

My great concern is not whether you have failed, but whether you are content with failure.

—Abraham Lincoln

Many of life's failures are people who did not realize how close they were to success when they gave up.

—Thomas Edison

You always pass failure on the way to success.

—Mickey Rooney

Failure is simply the opportunity to begin again, this time more intelligently.

—Henry Ford

The Road to Success

Failure meant a stripping away of the inessential. I stopped pretending to myself that I was anything other than I was and began diverting all my energy into finishing the only work that mattered to me.

—J.K. Rowling

* * *

Ever tried. Ever failed. No matter. Try again. Fail again. Fail better.

—Samuel Beckett

* * *

It's fine to celebrate success but it is more important to heed the lessons of failure.

—Bill Gates

* * *

What should happen when you make a mistake is this: you take your knocks, you learn your lessons, and then you move on.

—Ronald Reagan

Best Advice Ever

If you have made mistakes, even serious ones, there is always another chance for you. What we call failure is not the falling down, but the staying down.

—Mary Pickford

Once you have experienced a failure or a disappointment, once you've analyzed it and gotten the lessons out of it—dump it.

—Colin Powell

If you can't accept losing, you can't win.

—Vince Lombardi

I've missed more than 9,000 shots in my career. I've lost almost 300 games. 26 times, I've been trusted to take the game-winning shot and missed. I've failed over and over and over again in my life. And that is why I succeed.

—Michael Jordan

The Road to Success

It is impossible to live without failing at something, unless you live so cautiously that you might as well not have lived at all—in which case, you fail by default.

—J.K. Rowling

* * *

A lot of people ask me, "How did you have the courage to walk up to record labels when you were 12 or 13 and jump right into the music industry?" It's because I knew I could never feel the kind of rejection that I felt in middle school. Because in the music industry, if they're gonna say no to you, at least they're gonna be polite about it.

—Taylor Swift

* * *

To invent, you need a good imagination and a pile of junk.

—Thomas Edison

* * *

Winning is important to me, but what brings me joy is the experience of being fully engaged in whatever I'm doing.

—Phil Jackson

Best Advice Ever

You've got to take the initiative and play your game. In a decisive set, confidence is the difference.

—Chris Evert

That is the American story. People, just like you, following their passions, determined to meet the times on their own terms. They weren't doing it for the money. Their titles weren't fancy. But they changed the course of history and so can you.

—Barack Obama

You can't connect the dots looking forward; you can only connect them looking backwards. So you have to trust that the dots will somehow connect in your future. You have to trust in something—your gut, destiny, life, karma, whatever. This approach has never let me down, and it has made all the difference in my life.

—Steve Jobs

Follow what you are genuinely passionate about and let that guide you to your destination.

—Diane Sawyer

LIFE'S A CHALLENGE

Best Advice Ever

Life brings sorrows and joys alike. It is what a man does with them—not what they do to him—that is the true test of his mettle.

—Theodore Roosevelt

* * *

There is always inequity in life. Some men are killed in a war and some men are wounded, and some men never leave the country. . . . Life is unfair.

—John F. Kennedy

* * *

Nothing that is worthwhile is ever easy.

—Indira Gandhi

* * *

There are always two choices, two paths to take. One is easy. And its only reward is that it's easy.

—Anonymous

* * *

I learned that courage was not the absence of fear, but the triumph over it. The brave man is not he who does not feel afraid, but he who conquers that fear.

—Nelson Mandela

Life's a Challenge

I have learned over the years that when one's mind is made up, this diminishes fear; knowing what must be done does away with fear.

—Rosa Parks

* * *

Where I grew up—I grew up on the north side of Akron, lived in the projects. So those scared and lonely nights—that's every night. You hear a lot of police sirens, you hear a lot of gunfire. Things that you don't want your kids to hear growing up.

—LeBron James

* * *

When you get into a tight place and it seems you can't go on, hold on, for that's just the place and the time that the tide will turn.

—Harriet Beecher Stowe

* * *

The ultimate measure of a man is not where he stands in moments of comfort and convenience, but where he stands at times of challenge and controversy.

—Martin Luther King, Jr.

Best Advice Ever

You can't be brave if you've only had wonderful things happen to you.

—Mary Tyler Moore

✦ ✦ ✦

I have never in my life envied a human being who led an easy life; I have envied a great many people who led difficult lives and led them well.

—Theodore Roosevelt

✦ ✦ ✦

Sometimes life is going to hit you in the head with a brick. Don't lose faith.

—Steve Jobs

✦ ✦ ✦

Not everything happens for a reason. Sometimes life just sucks.

—Lorde

✦ ✦ ✦

Whatever someone did to you in the past has no power over the present.

—Oprah Winfrey

Life's a Challenge

When the going gets tough, the tough get going.

—Anonymous

* * *

Just when the caterpillar thought the world was over, it became a butterfly.

—English proverb

* * *

One of the lessons that I grew up with was to always stay true to yourself and never let what somebody else says distract you from your goals. And so when I hear about negative and false attacks, I really don't invest any energy in them, because I know who I am.

—Michelle Obama

* * *

Turn your wounds into wisdom.

—Oprah Winfrey

* * *

The mind is its own place, and in itself
Can make a Heaven of Hell, a Hell of Heaven.

—John Milton

Best Advice Ever

I have spent most of my life worrying about things that have never happened.

—**Mark Twain**

I've been on the floor and I've been heartbroken. I didn't know how I was going to stand up. But I just gave it time.

—**Sandra Bullock**

The reality is: sometimes you lose. And you're never too good to lose. You're never too big to lose. You're never too smart to lose. It happens.

—**Beyoncé**

Although the world is full of suffering, it is also full of the overcoming of it.

—**Helen Keller**

You gain strength, courage, and confidence by every experience in which you really stop to look fear in the face.

—**Eleanor Roosevelt**

Life's a Challenge

Smooth seas do not make skillful sailors.

—African proverb

When you get to the end of your rope, tie a knot and hang on.

—Franklin D. Roosevelt

It is a common experience that a problem difficult at night is resolved in the morning after the committee of sleep has worked on it.

—John Steinbeck

It's always darkest just before the day dawneth.

—Thomas Fuller

If there were no tribulation, there would be no rest; if there were no winter, there would be no summer.

—St. John Chrysostom

Best Advice Ever

Life is not meant to be easy, my child; but take courage—it can be delightful.

—George Bernard Shaw

* * *

I've learned that no matter what happens, or how bad it seems today, life does go on, and it will be better tomorrow.

—Maya Angelou

HAPPINESS IS . . .

Best Advice Ever

There is only one happiness in life, to love and be loved.

—George Sand

It is neither wealth nor splendor, but tranquility and occupation, which give happiness.

—Thomas Jefferson

The road to happiness lies in two simple principles: find out what it is that interests you and that you can do well, and when you find it, put your whole soul into it—every bit of energy and ambition and natural ability you have.

—John D. Rockefeller III

Personal happiness lies in knowing that life is not a checklist of acquisition or achievement. Your qualifications are not your life.

—J.K. Rowling

Happiness Is...

You're happiest while you're making the greatest contribution.

—Robert F. Kennedy

* * *

Happiness is when what you think, what you say, and what you do are in harmony.

—Mahatma Gandhi

* * *

From the greatest to the smallest, happiness and usefulness are largely found in the same soul, and the joy of life is won in its deepest and truest sense only by those who have not shirked life's burdens.

—Theodore Roosevelt

* * *

It is the ultimate luxury to combine passion and contribution. It's also a very clear path to happiness.

—Sheryl Sandberg

Best Advice Ever

Those who are happiest are those who do the most for others.

—Booker T. Washington

* * *

Happiness is like a butterfly. The more you chase it, the more it will elude you. But if you turn your attention to other things, it comes and softly sits on your shoulder.

—Anonymous

* * *

When one door of happiness closes, another opens; but often we look so long at the closed door that we do not see the one which has been opened for us.

—Helen Keller

* * *

We find delight in the beauty and happiness of children that makes the heart too big for the body.

—Ralph Waldo Emerson

Happiness Is...

Get a life in which you are not alone. Find people you love, and who love you. And remember that love is not leisure; it is work. Each time you look at your diploma, remember that you are still a student, still learning how to best treasure your connection to others. Pick up the phone. Send an e-mail. Write a letter. Kiss your Mom. Hug your Dad.

—Anna Quindlen

Life is made up of small pleasures. Happiness is made up of those tiny successes. The big ones come too infrequently. And if you don't collect all these tiny successes, the big ones don't really mean anything.

—Norman Lear

Just the knowledge that a good book is awaiting one at the end of a long day makes that day happier.

—Kathleen Norris

Best Advice Ever

What makes me happy is just curling up in with my mom in her bed and watching a marathon of *CSI* and *Grey's Anatomy* episodes with pints of ice cream.

—Taylor Swift

The best way to cheer yourself up is to try to cheer somebody else up.

—Mark Twain

Nothing can bring you to happiness but yourself.

—Ralph Waldo Emerson

We tend to forget that happiness doesn't come as a result of getting something we don't have, but rather of recognizing and appreciating what we do have.

—Frederick Koenig

Joy is what happens to us when we allow ourselves to recognize how good things really are.

—Marianne Williamson

Happiness Is...

The real things haven't changed. It is still best to be honest and truthful; to make the most of what we have; to be happy with simple pleasures; and have courage when things go wrong.

—**Laura Ingalls Wilder**

HAVE FUN!

Best Advice Ever

"Have fun" is my message. Be silly. You're allowed to be silly. There's nothing wrong with it.

—Jimmy Fallon

* * *

Children's games are hardly games. Children are never more serious than when they play.

—Montaigne

* * *

Play is often talked about as if it were a relief from serious learning. But for children play is serious learning. Play is really the work of childhood.

—Fred Rogers

* * *

I like nonsense, it wakes up the brain cells. Fantasy is a necessary ingredient in living, it's a way of looking at life through the wrong end of a telescope. Which is what I do, and that enables you to laugh at life's realities.

—Theodor Geisel

Have Fun!

When I get up in the morning and put on a pink or a green wig, I see myself as a piece of animation. It lets me be the person I want to be, a person who's not embarrassed to have fun.

—**Nicki Minaj**

* * *

The human race has one really effective weapon, and that is laughter.

—**Mark Twain**

* * *

I think one of my favorite things to do is just lock myself up in a small room and listen to music and watch films for a day. Also I just like seeing my friends. We have pizza parties which means I get four friends round, we eat a pizza and we're really lazy and we play PlayStation.

—**Daniel Radcliffe**

* * *

It's not like I'm hanging out at shopping malls or going to celebrity golf tournaments. I'm so in my own little world. I got my dog, my music, my brother, a couple of friends.

—**Jared Leto**

Best Advice Ever

I do love to shop. But I'm a social shopper. I like to do it while hanging out with my friends. Some of them hate shopping because they treat it like something you have to plan, like a grocery list. But if I'm out and I pass a store, I just pop in.

—Nicole Richie

We all started snowboarding in the beginning as a family just to be closer together, go on trips. It was our soccer, but instead of Dad yelling at me from the sideline he is there riding with me and hitting the jumps even before I am hitting them.

—Shaun White

Climb the mountains and get their good tidings. Nature's peace will flow into you as sunshine flows into trees. The winds will blow their own freshness into you, and the storms their energy, while cares will drop off like autumn leaves.

—John Muir

Have Fun!

You gotta have fun. Regardless of how you look at it, we're playing a game. It's a business, it's our job, but I don't think you can do well unless you're having fun.

— **Derek Jeter**

* * *

When you have confidence, you can have a lot of fun. And when you have fun, you can do amazing things.

— **Joe Namath**

* * *

To love what you do and feel that it matters—how could anything be more fun?

— **Katharine Graham**

* * *

People rarely succeed unless they have fun in what they are doing.

— **Dale Carnegie**

Best Advice Ever

Somewhere behind the athlete you've become and the hours of practice and the coaches who have pushed you is a little girl who fell in love with the game and never looked back . . . play for her.

—**Mia Hamm**

* * *

When you play, play hard. When you work, don't play at all.

—**Theodore Roosevelt**

THE WORLD WE LIVE IN

Best Advice Ever

Kids deserve the right to think that they can change the world.

—**Lois Lowry**

* * *

We must be the change we wish to see in the world.

—**Mahatma Gandhi**

* * *

Never doubt that a small group of thoughtful committed citizens can change the world; indeed, it is the only thing that ever has.

—**Margaret Mead**

* * *

Is the rich world aware of how four billion of the six billion live? If we were aware, we would want to help out, we'd want to get involved.

—**Bill Gates**

* * *

I've always respected those who tried to change the world for the better, rather than just complain about it.

—**Michael Bloomberg**

The World We Live In

No one person has to do it all but if each one of us follow our heart and our own inclinations we will find the small things that we can do to create a sustainable future and a healthy environment.

—John Denver

* * *

It is every man's obligation to put back into the world at least the equivalent of what he takes out of it.

—Albert Einstein

* * *

Injustice anywhere is a threat to justice everywhere.

—Martin Luther King, Jr.

* * *

When the power of love overcomes the love of power, the world will be at peace.

—Bob Marley

* * *

The world is more malleable than you think and it's waiting for you to hammer it into shape.

—Bono

Best Advice Ever

We must learn to live together as brothers or perish together as fools.

—**Martin Luther King, Jr.**

* * *

I want my life to be about more than just fame or jewelry or parties. Hip-hop has the power to change the world. I am here to lead by example.

—**Sean Combs**

* * *

Let no one be discouraged by the belief that there is nothing one person can do against the enormous array of the world's ills, misery, ignorance, and violence. Few will have the greatness to bend history, but each of us can work to change a small portion of events. And in the total of all those acts will be written the history of a generation.

—**Robert F. Kennedy**

* * *

My country is the world, and my religion is to do good.

—**Thomas Paine**

The World We Live In

Let us remember: One book, one pen, one child, and one teacher can change the world.

—Malala Yousafzai

* * *

You see things; and say "Why?" But I dream things that never were; and I say "Why not?"

—George Bernard Shaw

* * *

Every great dream begins with a dreamer. Always remember, you have within you the strength, the patience, and the passion to reach for the stars to change the world.

—Harriet Tubman

* * *

How wonderful it is that nobody need wait a single moment before starting to improve the world.

—Anne Frank

EPIC ADVICE

Best Advice Ever

Surround yourself with only people who are going to lift you higher.

—**Oprah Winfrey**

' ' '

Keep away from people who try to belittle your ambitions. Small people always do that, but the really great make you feel that you, too, can become great.

—**Mark Twain**

' ' '

Surround yourself with good people. People who are going to be honest with you and look out for your best interests.

—**Derek Jeter**

' ' '

I want you to find strength in your diversity. Let the fact that you are black or yellow or white be a source of pride and inspiration to you. Draw strength from it. Let it be someone else's problem, but never yours. Never hide behind it or use it as an excuse for not doing your best.

—**Colin Powell**

Epic Advice

In any situation, the best thing you can do is the right thing; the next best thing you can do is the wrong thing; the worst thing you can do is nothing.

—Theodore Roosevelt

In matters of style, swim with the current; in matters of principle, stand like a rock.

—Thomas Jefferson

Have patience with all things, but chiefly have patience with yourself. Do not lose courage in considering your own imperfections, but instantly set about remedying them—every day begin the task anew.

—St. Francis de Sales

Everyone has inside of her a piece of good news. The good news is that you don't know how great you can be! How much you can love! What you can accomplish! And what your potential is!

—Anne Frank

Best Advice Ever

Be congruent, be authentic, be your true self.

—**Mahatma Gandhi**

* * *

I don't have to be perfect. All I have to do is show up and enjoy the messy, imperfect, and beautiful journey of my life. It's a trip more wonderful than I could have imagined.

—**Kerry Washington**

* * *

The thing that is really hard, and really amazing, is giving up on being perfect and beginning the work of becoming yourself.

—**Anna Quindlen**

* * *

Don't compromise yourself. You are all you've got.

—**Janis Joplin**

* * *

Deal with yourself as an individual worthy of respect, and make everyone else deal with you the same way.

—**Nikki Giovanni**

Epic Advice

When people show you who they are, believe them.

—Maya Angelou

✦ ✧ ✦

Be nice to nerds. Chances are you'll end up working for one.

—Bill Gates

✦ ✧ ✦

Know the true value of time; snatch, seize, and enjoy every moment of it. No idleness, no laziness, no procrastination; never put off till tomorrow what you can do today.

—Lord Chesterfield

✦ ✧ ✦

Nine-tenths of wisdom consists in being wise in time.

—Theodore Roosevelt

✦ ✧ ✦

When I dare to be powerful, to use my strength in the service of my vision, then it becomes less and less important whether I am afraid.

—Audre Lorde

Best Advice Ever

Trust your hunches. They're usually based on facts filed away just below the conscious level.

—Joyce Brothers

* * *

Life was meant to be lived, and curiosity must be kept alive. One must never, for whatever reason, turn his back on life.

—Eleanor Roosevelt

* * *

If you're offered a seat on a rocket ship, don't ask what seat! Just get on.

—Sheryl Sandberg

* * *

Life is what happens to you while you're busy making other plans.

—John Lennon

* * *

There are three ingredients in the good life: learning, earning, and yearning.

—Christopher Morley

Figuring out who you are is the whole point of the human experience.

—Anna Quindlen

* * *

Your time is limited, so don't waste it living someone else's life. Don't be trapped by dogma—which is living with the results of other people's thinking. Don't let the noise of other's opinions drown out your own inner voice. And most important, have the courage to follow your heart and intuition. They somehow already know what you truly want to become. Everything else is secondary.

—Steve Jobs

* * *

Find a group of people who challenge and inspire you, spend a lot of time with them, and it will change your life.

—Amy Poehler

* * *

If you are interested in something, no matter what it is, go at it at full speed ahead. Embrace it with both arms, hug it, love it and above all become passionate about it.

—Roald Dahl

Best Advice Ever

At the end of your life, you will never regret not having passed one more test, not winning one more verdict, or not closing one more deal. You will regret time not spent with a husband, a friend, a child, or a parent.

—Barbara Bush

* * *

The future depends entirely on what each of us does every day.

—Gloria Steinem

* * *

Take care of this moment.

—Mahatma Gandhi

* * *

The future belongs to those who believe in the beauty of their dreams.

—Eleanor Roosevelt

* * *

So many of our dreams at first seem impossible, then they seem improbable, and then when we summon the will, they soon become inevitable.

—Christopher Reeve

Epic Advice

A ship in port is safe, but that is not what ships are for. Sail out to sea and do new things.

—Grace Hopper

Do something every day that you don't want to do; this is the golden rule for acquiring the habit of doing your duty without pain.

—Mark Twain

If you don't go after what you want, you'll never have it. If you don't ask, the answer is always no. If you don't step forward, you're always in the same place.

—Nora Roberts

Be thankful for what you have; you'll end up having more. If you concentrate on what you don't have, you will never, ever have enough.

—Oprah Winfrey

Best Advice Ever

Dreaming, after all, is a form of planning.

—Gloria Steinem

* * *

I stand for freedom of expression, doing what you believe in, and going after your dreams.

—Madonna

* * *

I like the dreams of the future better than the history of the past.

—Thomas Jefferson

* * *

Life isn't about finding yourself. Life is about creating yourself.

—George Bernard Shaw

* * *

Above all watch with glittering eyes the whole world around you because the greatest secrets are always hidden in the most unlikely places.

—Roald Dahl

Epic Advice

The truth is you don't know what is going to happen tomorrow. Life is a crazy ride, and nothing is guaranteed.

—Eminem

* * *

So with imagination, ingenuity and audacity, explore, discover, change the world. And have fun while you're at it. Always take time out to love and to live. You're going to be busy, but never forget friends and family.

—Daniel S. Goldin

* * *

Take care of your body. It's the only place you have to live.

—Jim Rohn

* * *

Go confidently in the direction of your dreams. Live the life you have imagined.

—Henry David Thoreau

* * *

A life is not important except in the impact it has on other lives.

—Jackie Robinson

Best Advice Ever

Contributors

Kareem Abdul-Jabbar (b. 1947) — American basketball player, coach, broadcaster, and writer

Alfred Adler (1870–1937) — Austrian philosopher and psychiatrist

Aesop (620–564 B.C.) — Greek fabulist

Mohamed Al-Fayed (b. 1929) — Egyptian business magnate

Louisa May Alcott (1832–1888) — American novelist

Muhammad Ali (b. 1942) — American boxer and philanthropist

Maya Angelou (b. 1928–2014) — American writer and poet

Jennifer Aniston (b. 1969) — American actress and producer

Aristotle (384–322 B.C.) — Greek philosopher

Arthur Ashe (1943–1993) — American tennis player and humanitarian

Jane Austen (1775–1817) — English novelist

Francis Bacon (1561–1626) — English Renaissance statesman, philosopher, and scientist

Ireland Baldwin (b. 1995) — American model

Steve Ballmer (b. 1956) — American businessman

Dave Barry (b. 1947) — American writer

Samuel Beckett (1906–1989) — Irish writer

Beyoncé (b. 1981) — American singer-songwriter, record producer, and actress

Michael Bloomberg (b. 1942) — American business magnate, politician, and philanthropist

Judy Blume (b. 1938) — American writer

Erma Bombeck (1927–1996) — American humorist and writer

Bono (b. 1960) — Irish musician, singer-songwriter, and philanthropist

Nadia Boulanger (1887–1979) — French composer, conductor, and teacher

Tom Brady (b. 1977) — American football player

Stewart Brand (b. 1938) — American writer and editor

Adrien Brody (b. 1973) — American actor

Joyce Brothers (1927–2013) — American psychologist and columnist

Contributors

Andrew Brown (b. 1955) — English journalist, editor, and writer

Sandra Bullock (b. 1964) — American actress and producer

LeVar Burton (b. 1957) — American actor, director, producer, and writer

Leo Buscaglia (1924–1998) — American writer, motivational speaker, and professor

Barbara Bush (b. 1925) — Former first lady of the United States and humanitarian

Albert Camus (1913–1960) — French novelist, essayist, and dramatist

George Carlin (1937–2008) — American comedian, writer, and actor

Dale Carnegie (1888–1955) — American writer and lecturer

Jackie Chan (b. 1954) — Hong Kong actor, martial artist, director, producer, writer, stunt director, and performer

Charlie Chaplin (1889–1977) — English actor, comedian, filmmaker, and composer

Anton Chekhov (1860–1904) — Russian dramatist and writer

Lord Chesterfield (1694–1773) — English statesman and writer

Margaret Cho (b. 1968) — American comedian and actress

Deepak Chopra (b. 1947) — Indian-American writer and public speaker

St. John Chrysostom (c. 347–407) — Roman Catholic saint

Winston Churchill (1874–1965) — British statesman and prime minister

Madonna (b. 1958) — American singer-songwriter and actress

Cicero (106–43 B.C.) — Roman statesman, orator, and writer

Hillary Clinton (b. 1947) — American politician, former secretary of state, and former first lady of the United States

Paulo Coelho (b. 1947) — Brazilian novelist

Colette (1873–1954) — French novelist and performer

Sean Combs (b. 1969) — American rap artist, actor, producer, and entrepreneur

Anderson Cooper (b. 1967) — American journalist, writer, and television personality

Katie Couric (b. 1957) — American journalist, writer, and television personality

Quentin Crisp (1908–1999) — English writer, illustrator, and actor

e. e. Cummings (1894–1962) — American poet

Roald Dahl (1916–1990) — British writer

Best Advice Ever

John Denver (1943–1997) — American singer-songwriter, actor, activist, and humanitarian

Johnny Depp (b. 1963) — American actor, producer, and musician

Zooey Deschanel (b. 1980) — American actress and singer-songwriter

Barbara De Angelis (b. 1951) — American counselor, lecturer, and writer

Ellen DeGeneres (b. 1958) — American comedian, writer, and television host

St. Francis de Sales (1567–1622) — Roman Catholic saint

Emily Dickinson (1830–1886) — American poet

Benjamin Disraeli (1804–1881) — British politician, writer, and prime minister

Kevin Durant (b. 1988) — American basketball player

Michael Eric Dyson (b. 1958) — American academic, writer, and radio host

Amelia Earhart (1897–1937) — American aviator and writer

Marian Wright Edelman (b. 1939) — American children's rights activist

Thomas Edison (1847–1931) — American inventor

Zac Efron (b. 1987) — American actor and singer

Albert Einstein (1879–1955) — German-born American physicist

Charles W. Eliot (1834–1926) — American educator

George Eliot (1819–1880) — English novelist

T. S. Eliot (1888–1965) — American-born English poet, writer, and critic

Ralph Waldo Emerson (1803–1882) — American essayist and poet

Eminem (b. 1972) — American rapper

Chris Evert (b. 1954) — American tennis player, coach, and tennis commentator, and publisher

Jimmy Fallon (b. 1974) — American comedian and television host

Tina Fey (b. 1970) — American actress, writer, comedian, and producer

Harvey Fierstein (b. 1954) — American actor and playwright

Colin Firth (b. 1960) — English actor

F. Scott Fitzgerald (1896–1940) — American writer

Malcolm Forbes (1919–1990) — American publisher and business leader

Henry Ford (1863–1947) — American industrialist and the founder of the Ford Motor Company

Contributors

Megan Fox (b. 1986) — American actress

Pope Francis (b. 1936) — 266th pope of the Catholic Church

Anne Frank (1929–1945) — German diarist

Benjamin Franklin (1706–1790) — American statesman and philosopher

Northrop Frye (1912–1991) — Canadian literary critic and literary theorist

Thomas Fuller (1608–1661) — English clergyman and historian

Indira Gandhi (1917–1984) — prime minister of India

Mahatma Gandhi (1869–1948) — Indian nationalist leader

Bill Gates (b. 1955) — American business magnate, philanthropist, investor, and inventor

Melinda Gates (b. 1964) — American businesswoman and philanthropist

Theodor Geisel (a.k.a. Dr. Seuss) (1904–1991) — American writer, cartoonist, animator, publisher, and artist

Kahlil Gibran (1883–1931) — Lebanese novelist, poet, and artist

Nikki Giovanni (b. 1943) — American poet and writer, activist, and educator

Goethe (Johann Wolfgang von) (1749–1832) — German poet and dramatist

Daniel S. Goldin (b. 1940) — American mechanical engineer and NASA administrator

Katharine Graham (1917–2001) — American newspaper publisher

Ariana Grande (b. 1993) — American singer and actress

Ulysses S. Grant (1822–1885) — Eighteenth president of the United States

John Green (b. 1977) — American novelist and blogger

Wayne Gretzky (b. 1961) — Canadian hockey player and coach

Alex Haley (1921–1992) — American writer

John Hamm (b. 1971) — American actor, director, and producer

Mia Hamm (b. 1972) — American soccer player and writer

Thich Nhat Hanh (b.1926) — Vietnamese Buddhist monk, peace activist, and writer

Anne Hathaway (b. 1982) — American actress and singer

Kevin Heath (b. 1950) — Australian football player

Robert A. Heinlein (1907–1988) — American science-fiction writer

Ernest Hemingway (1899–1961) — American writer and journalist

Best Advice Ever

Grace Hopper (1906–1992) — American military and computer scientist

Edgar Watson Howe (1853–1937) — American novelist and editor

Zora Neale Hurston (1891–1960) — American writer, folklorist, and anthropologist

Phil Jackson (b. 1945) — American basketball executive, former basketball player, and coach

Henry James (1811–1882) — American philosopher

Kevin James (b. 1965) — American comedian, actor, writer, and producer

LeBron James (b. 1984) — American basketball player

Thomas Jefferson (1743–1826) — Third president of the United States

Derek Jeter (b. 1974) — American baseball player

Steve Jobs (1955–2011) — American entrepreneur, inventor, and co-founder, chairman, and CEO of Apple, Inc.

Nick Jonas (b. 1992) — American singer-songwriter, musician, and actor

Ben Jonson (1572–1637) — English playwright and poet

Janis Joplin (1943–1970) — American singer-songwriter

Michael Jordan (b. 1963) — American basketball player, businessman, writer

Joseph Joubert (1754–1824) — French moralist and essayist

Mindy Kaling (b. 1979) — American actress, writer, producer, and director

Diane Keaton (b. 1946) — American actress, director, producer, and writer

Helen Keller (1880–1968) — American writer, activist, and educator

Caroline Kennedy (b. 1957) — American writer, attorney, and United States ambassador

John F. Kennedy (1917–1963) — Thirty-fifth president of the United States

Robert F. Kennedy (1925–1968) — American politician and attorney general

Billie Jean King (b. 1943) — American tennis player

Martin Luther King, Jr. (1929–1968) — American clergyman and civil rights leader

Stephen King (b. 1947) — American novelist

Frederick Koenig (1774–1833) — German inventor

Rabbi Harold Kushner (b. 1935) — American rabbi and writer

Doug Larson (b. 1926) — American journalist

Contributors

Queen Latifah (b. 1970) — American singer/songwriter, rap artist, model, and actress; born Dana Elaine Owens

Sara Lawrence-Lightfoot (b. 1944) — American sociologist

Norman Lear (b. 1922) — American television writer and producer

Robert E. Lee (1807–1870) — American Confederate general, president of Washington and Lee University

John Lennon (1940–1980) — English musician, singer-songwriter, writer, record producer, and social activist

Jared Leto (b. 1971) — American actor, singer-songwriter, director, activist

Doris Lessing (1919–2013) — English writer

C. S. Lewis (1898–1963) — Irish-born novelist and essayist

Abraham Lincoln (1809–1865) — Sixteenth president of the United States

Vince Lombardi (1913–1970) — American football coach

Henry Wadsworth Longfellow (1807–1882) — American poet

Audre Lorde (1934–1992) — American novelist and writer

Lorde (b. 1996) — New Zealand singer-songwriter

Demi Lovato (b. 1992) — American singer-songwriter and actress

Lois Lowry (b. 1937) — American writer

Martin Luther (1483–1546) — German Reformation leader

James Madison (1751–1836) — Fourth president of the United States

Nelson Mandela (1918–2013) — South African political leader, activist, humanitarian, philanthropist, and lawyer

Bob Marley (1945–1981) — Jamaican reggae singer-songwriter, musician, and activist

Margaret Mead (1901–1978) — American cultural anthropologist and writer

Thomas Merton (1915–1968) — American writer and Trappist monk

Henry Miller (1891–1980) — American writer

John Milton (1608–1674) — English poet

Nicki Minaj (b. 1982) — American rapper and singer-songwriter

Nancy Mitford (1904–1973) — English novelist, biographer, and journalist

Michel de Montaigne (1533–1592) — French essayist

Mary Tyler Moore (b. 1936) — American actress

Best Advice Ever

Christopher Morley (1890–1957) — American writer and editor

John Muir (1838–1914) — Scottish-born American naturalist

Joe Namath (b. 1943) — American football player and actor

Anaïs Nin (1903–1977) — French-born American writer

Kathleen Norris (1880–1966) — American novelist and newspaper columnist

Sandra Day O'Connor (b. 1930) — American jurist and first woman appointed to United States Supreme Court

Georgia O'Keeffe (1887–1986) — American painter

Barack Obama (b. 1961) — Forty-fourth president of the United States

Michelle Obama (b. 1964) — American lawyer, writer, and first African-American First Lady of the United States

Thomas Paine (1737–1809) — American politician, philosopher, and writer

Gwyneth Paltrow (b. 1972) — American actress, singer, and writer

Dorothy Parker (1893–1967) — American poet and writer

Rosa Parks (1913–2005) — American civil rights activist

St. Paul (c. 3–65) — Early Christian apostle and martyr

Katy Perry (b. 1984) — American singer, songwriter, and actress

Pablo Picasso (1881–1973) — Spanish artist, poet, and playwright

Mary Pickford (1892–1979) — Canadian actress and film studio co-founder

Pink (b. 1979) — American singer-songwriter and actress

St. Padre Pio (1887–1968) — Roman Catholic saint

Plato (ca. 428–348) — Greek philosopher and writer

Plutarch (ca. 46–122) — Greek philosopher and writer

Amy Poehler (b. 1971) — American actress, comedian, writer, and producer

Alexander Pope (1688–1744) — English poet

Natalie Portman (b. 1981) — American actress

Colin Powell (b. 1937) — American retired four-star general in United States Army and former secretary of state

J. B. Priestly (1894–1984) — English writer and broadcaster

Marcel Proust (1871–1922) — French novelist, essayist, and critic

Anna Quindlen (b. 1952) — American writer and journalist

Contributors

Daniel Radcliffe (b. 1989) — English actor

Ronald Reagan (1911–2004) — Fortieth president of the United States

Christopher Reeve (1952–2004) — American actor, director, producer, writer, and activist

Keanu Reeves (b. 1964) — Canadian actor, director, and musician

Nicole Richie (b. 1981) — American fashion designer, actress, and writer

Nora Roberts (b. 1950) — American novelist

Julia Roberts (b. 1967) — American actress and producer

Jackie Robinson (1919–1972) — American baseball player and first African-American to play in the Major Leagues

John D. Rockefeller III (1906–1978) — American philanthropist

Fred Rogers (1928–2003) — American educator, clergyman, and television host

Jim Rohn (1930–2009) — American entrepreneur, writer, and motivational speaker

Mickey Rooney (1920–2014) —American actor

Eleanor Roosevelt (1884–1962) — American humanitarian, political activist, and longest-serving first lady of the United States

Franklin D. Roosevelt (1882–1945) — Thirty-second president of the United States

Theodore Roosevelt (1858–1919) — Twenty-sixth president of the United States

J.K. Rowling (b. 1965) — English novelist

Bertrand Russell (1872–1970) — English mathematician and philosopher

Sheryl Sandberg (b. 1969) — American business executive and writer

Diane Sawyer (b. 1945) — American broadcast journalist

George Sand (1804–1876) — French writer

Albert Schweitzer (1875–1965) — German-born French theologian, humanitarian, organist, and medical doctor

George Bernard Shaw (1856–1950) — Irish playwright and author

Logan Pearsall Smith (1865–1946) — American-born British essayist and critic

Margaret Chase Smith (1897–1995) — American politician

Patti Smith (b. 1946) — American poet, singer, songwriter

Socrates (470–399 b.c.) — Greek philosopher

Best Advice Ever

Sonia Sotomayor (b. 1954) — United States Supreme Court Justice and first Hispanic to serve on the Court

Nicholas Sparks (b. 1965) — American novelist, screenwriter, and producer

Steven Spielberg (b. 1946) — American film director, screenwriter, producer, and philanthropist

Bruce Springsteen (b. 1949) — American singer-songwriter and musician

John Steinbeck (1902–1968) — American writer

Gloria Steinem (b. 1934) — American writer, journalist, and political and social activist

Robert Louis Stevenson (1850–1894) — Scottish writer

Jon Stewart (b. 1962) — American political satirist, television host, writer, producer, and director

Harriet Beecher Stowe (1811–1896) — American writer and abolitionist

Taylor Swift (b. 1989) — American singer-songwriter

William D. Tammeus (b. 1945?) — American journalist

Mother Teresa (1910–1997) — Albanian-born Roman Catholic nun, declared Blessed in 2003, who devoted her life to the poor of Calcutta

Henry David Thoreau (1817–1862) — American writer and philosopher

Harriet Tubman (1820–1913) — American abolitionist

Desmond Tutu (b. 1931) — South African social rights activist and retired Anglican bishop

Mark Twain (1835–1910) — American writer and lecturer

Lao Tzu (c. 6th century B.C.) — Chinese poet and philosopher

Carrie Underwood (b. 1983) — American singer-songwriter

John Updike (1932–2009) — American writer

Jim Valvano (1946–1993) — American college basketball coach and broadcaster

St. John Vianney (1786–1859) — Roman Catholic saint

Margaret Walker (1915–1998) — American poet and writer

Booker T. Washington (1856–1915) — American educator, writer, and prominent African-American leader

Denzel Washington (b. 1954) — American actor, director, and producer

George Washington (1732–1799) — First president of the United States

Contributors

Kerry Washington (b. 1977) — American actress

Shaun White (b. 1986) — American snowboarder, skateboarder, and Olympic gold medalist

Walt Whitman (1819–1892) — American poet

Elie Wiesel (b. 1928) — Romanian-born American writer, professor, political activist, and humanitarian

Oscar Wilde (1854–1900) — Irish writer

Laura Ingalls Wilder (1867–1957) — American writer

Serena Williams (b. 1981) — American tennis player

Marianne Williamson (b. 1952) — American spiritual teacher, writer, and lecturer

Woodrow Wilson (1856–1924) — Twenty-eighth president of the United States

August Wilson, Jr. (1945– 2005) — American playwright

Oprah Winfrey (b. 1954) — American media mogul, talk-show host, actress, and philanthropist

Tobias Wolff (b. 1945) — American writer

Tiger Woods (b. 1975) — American golfer

Virginia Woolf (1882–1941) — English writer

Malcolm X (1925–1965) — American religious leader and political activist

William Butler Yeats (1865–1939) — Irish poet and playwright

Malala Yousafzai (b. 1997) — Pakistani activist for the education of girls and youngest recipient of the Nobel Prize

Mark Zuckerberg (b. 1984) — American Internet entrepreneur, and co-founder, chairman, and CEO of Facebook, Inc.